WWW.APEXEDITIONS.COM

Copyright © 2026 by Apex Editions, Mendota Heights, MN 55120. All rights reserved. No part of this book may be reproduced or utilized in any form or by any means without written permission from the publisher.

Apex is distributed by North Star Editions:
sales@northstareditions.com | 888-417-0195

Produced for Apex by Red Line Editorial.

Photographs ©: Noah Berger/AP Images, cover, 1; Shutterstock Images, 4–5, 8–9, 10–11, 12–13, 16–17, 18–19, 22–23, 26–27, 29, 32–33, 36–37, 38–39, 40–41, 44–45, 50–51, 56–57, 58; NOAA, 6–7; iStockphoto, 14–15, 52–53; David Goldman/AP Images, 20–21; Forest History Society, Durham, NC, 24–25; Ben Smegelsky/NASA, 30–31; Justin Sullivan/Getty Images News/Getty Images, 34–35; Matthias Bein/dpa picture alliance/Alamy Live News/Alamy, 42–43; Chip Somodevilla/Getty Images News/Getty Images, 46–47; Joshua Stevens/NASA, 49; Mario Tama/Getty Images News/Getty Images, 54–55

**Library of Congress Control Number: 2025930911**

**ISBN**
979-8-89250-665-6 (hardcover)
979-8-89250-700-4 (ebook pdf)
979-8-89250-683-0 (hosted ebook)

Printed in the United States of America
Mankato, MN
082025

# NOTE TO PARENTS AND EDUCATORS

Apex books are designed to build literacy skills in striving readers. Exciting, high-interest content attracts and holds readers' attention. The text is carefully leveled to allow students to achieve success quickly.

# TABLE OF CONTENTS

Chapter 1

## FOREST FIRE  4

Chapter 2

## ALL ABOUT WILDFIRES  10

Chapter 3

## EARLY HISTORY  21

That's Wild!

## CULTURAL BURNS  28

Chapter 4

## FORECASTING FIRES  30

Chapter 5

## FIGHTING FIRES  40

That's Wild!

## 2018 CAMP FIRE  48

Chapter 6

## PREVENTING FUTURE FIRES  50

TIMELINE • 59
COMPREHENSION QUESTIONS • 60
GLOSSARY • 62
TO LEARN MORE • 63
ABOUT THE AUTHOR • 63
INDEX • 64

## Chapter 1

# FOREST FIRE

Crew members board a plane. They work for the United States Forest Service (USFS). The plane flies above a Colorado forest. One of the crew members sees smoke. He reports it over his radio. Then, scientists use a satellite to look at the area.

Wildfire smoke can travel thousands of miles.

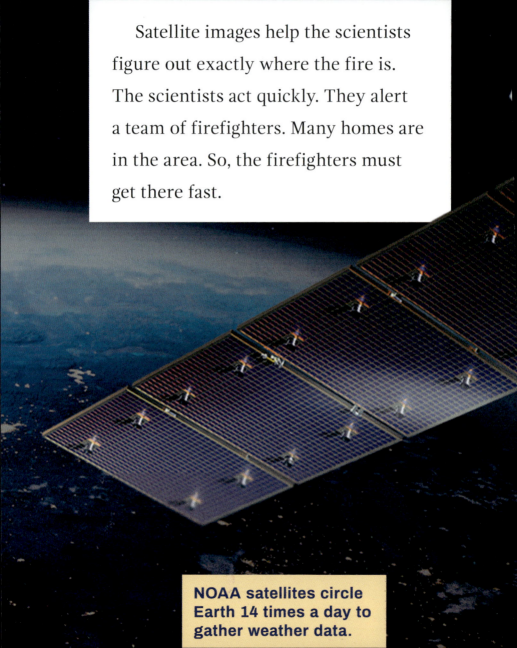

Satellite images help the scientists figure out exactly where the fire is. The scientists act quickly. They alert a team of firefighters. Many homes are in the area. So, the firefighters must get there fast.

**NOAA satellites circle Earth 14 times a day to gather weather data.**

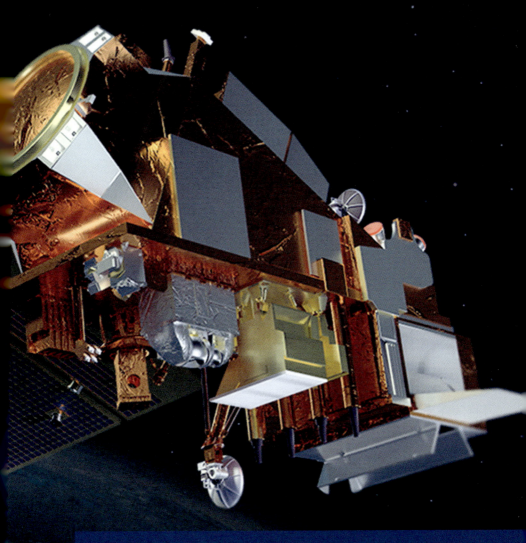

## FINDING FIRES

The National Oceanic and Atmospheric Administration (NOAA) is a government group. This group studies weather. Some of its satellites are used to find wildfires. A computer program scans the satellite photos. The program can figure out a fire's size and temperature. Scientists can also find out if a fire will spread quickly.

About 150 firefighters get to work. Airplanes and helicopters attack the fire from above. Fire trucks help on the ground. Firefighters use bulldozers to clear land. They also use hoses to shoot water at the flames. Within a few days, they contain the fire. The people and homes in the area are safe.

Planes drop water or chemical dust to stop fires.

**Chapter 2**

# ALL ABOUT WILDFIRES

Wildfires are unplanned, unwanted blazes. They burn in natural areas. Wildfires often spread quickly. Large blazes can move over thousands of acres. Millions of acres burn each year.

About 70,000 wildfires occur in the United States each year.

**Human activity is seven times more likely to cause wildfires than lightning strikes are.**

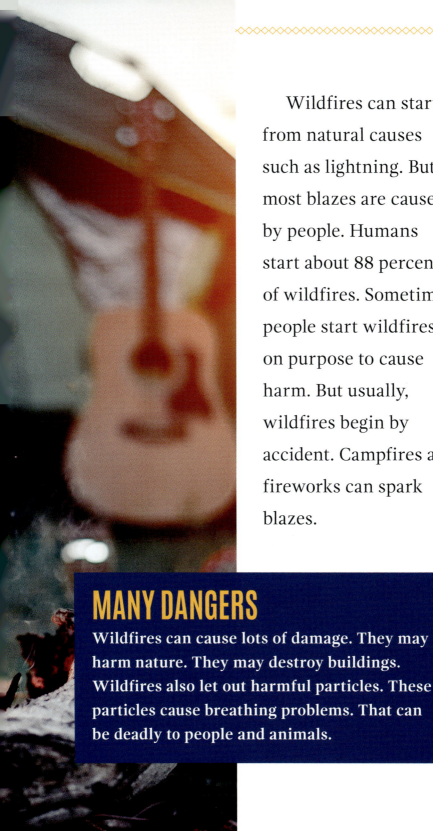

Wildfires can start from natural causes such as lightning. But most blazes are caused by people. Humans start about 88 percent of wildfires. Sometimes, people start wildfires on purpose to cause harm. But usually, wildfires begin by accident. Campfires and fireworks can spark blazes.

## MANY DANGERS

Wildfires can cause lots of damage. They may harm nature. They may destroy buildings. Wildfires also let out harmful particles. These particles cause breathing problems. That can be deadly to people and animals.

The sun's heat can spark wildfires.

Like all fires, wildfires have three ingredients. The first is fuel. Sticks and leaves burn easily. So, they can be the fuel. The second ingredient is air. Air provides oxygen. Fires need oxygen to burn. The third ingredient is heat. Together, these three ingredients are a recipe for a blaze.

## FIRE TRIANGLE

Fuel, air, and heat make up the fire triangle. Firefighters try to take out one part of the triangle. For example, they may remove fuel from an area. Then they can control the fire.

Wildfires can happen anywhere. However, they occur most often in forested or grassy areas. Wildfires are especially common in places with dry seasons.

Wildfires are most common in spring and summer. But they can happen any time of year.

## DROUGHTS

Parts of the western United States have long droughts. Droughts are also becoming more common in the Amazon Rainforest. These areas are seeing more and more blazes. Wildfires also occur in Indonesia and Australia. They even happen in the Arctic.

Crown fires often spread quickly. They can start from surface fires.

There are three types of wildfires. Surface fires are the weakest. They quickly burn up light fuels. These include dead leaves and branches. Surface fires usually don't kill older trees or root systems.

Crown fires are another type. They occur in the upper parts of trees. Crown fires may cause embers and sparks to fall. Flames can spread.

Ground fires are the rarest type. These blazes are strong and hot. They destroy all plants and animals in their path.

# EARLY HISTORY

**P**eople have been dealing with forest fires for thousands of years. Indigenous Americans carried out controlled burns. These burns kept forests healthy.

A member of the Yurok Tribe watches a controlled burn in California.

Today, people allow trees to grow closer together than they did in the past. So, fires can spread quickly between trees.

Over time, things changed. European colonists arrived in North America. The colonists didn't understand why Indigenous people carried out burns. The colonists thought the burns harmed forests. In 1850, California banned controlled burns. Colonists also cut down many trees to make buildings. They replanted the areas with thick groves.

## CHANGING THE FOREST

Controlled burns shaped forests. For example, parts of northern California used to be covered by water oak. Water oaks grow far apart. They made natural firebreaks. But without regular burns, tall pine trees blocked the sun. Water oaks could not grow.

In the early 1900s, workers built many lookout towers to watch for fires.

White settlers created wildfire control programs. The first official program in the United States formed in 1885. People tried to put out all fires no matter what. There were no controlled burns. So, dry fuel built up on the ground.

## BIG BLOWUP

In 1910, wildfires burned 3 million acres (1.2 million ha) in two days. The blazes went through Montana, Idaho, and Washington. Wildfire programs decided to work harder to stop all fires. In 1944, the USFS created a character named Smokey Bear. Smokey Bear warned people about wildfires.

25

Today, people use drip torches for controlled burns.

By the 1970s, wildfire programs started to see the problem with putting out all fires. So, they experimented with controlled burns. Over time, they started seeing benefits. Controlled fires burned up dried fuel. Also, new wildfires tended to stop when they reached areas that had burned recently. So, small burns stopped large wildfires.

## RISK MAPS

US scientists came up with a new system in 1972. They used math to figure out the risk of a wildfire in an area. Scientists used that information to create risk maps. These maps helped keep people safer.

# That's Wild!
# CULTURAL BURNS

US wildfire programs ignored Indigenous practices for more than 100 years. By the 2000s, that started to change. Park rangers started working with Indigenous groups.

One example happened in Yosemite National Park. In 2005, members of the Southern Sierra Miwuk Nation took part in a controlled burn. Members of the Tuolumne Band of Me-Wuk took part, too. The burn helped get rid of invasive plants. It also cleared up fuel. This burn helped prevent large fires in the future.

**Firefighters and Indigenous people burned invasive Himalayan blackberry.**

Chapter 4

# FORECASTING FIRES

Scientists try to predict future wildfires. The work starts long before blazes begin. Several factors affect the location and spread of wildfires. So, scientists start by collecting data.

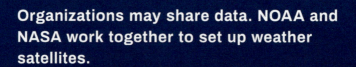

Organizations may share data. NOAA and NASA work together to set up weather satellites.

Weather stations measure and collect data. Temperature is one important condition. Fuel may get heated by the sun. Warmer temperatures make fuels ignite and burn faster. Wind is also important. It gives fires oxygen. And it causes blazes to spread.

## FAST FIRE

On November 6, 2024, a wildfire began in Southern California. That morning, winds blew more than 60 miles per hour (97 km/h). The wind spread embers. Some embers blew more than 2 miles (3.2 km). Within a day, the wildfire had grown to 20,000 acres (8,000 ha).

**Weather organizations have set up thousands of weather stations across the United States.**

**Human experts may need hours to predict a fire's path. But AI can do it in seconds.**

Scientists also study the moisture levels of fuel. To do so, they need measurements of temperature. They also need measurements of humidity and cloudiness. They put those measurements into math equations. The calculations let scientists figure out moisture levels of fuel.

## ARTIFICIAL INTELLIGENCE

Artificial intelligence (AI) programs help with wildfire forecasts. Some programs track fuel in an area. The programs consider current weather conditions. They also consider historical fire data. Then, the programs predict likely fire events over the next week.

Land features affect how quickly wildfires can spread. Fires tend to travel much faster uphill. That's because heat rises. A blaze can preheat and dry the fuel uphill. The steeper the slope, the faster the fire spreads.

## MAPPING THE LAND

Complex terrain is one of the biggest challenges in forecasting wildfires. Scientists try to create detailed 3D maps. The maps help scientists learn where fires will spread. To create maps, scientists may use lidar. Lidar is a sensor. It takes measurements using lasers.

**Drones can carry lidar sensors above forests.**

All that data helps scientists create better risk maps. Then, officials can send firefighters to risky areas. Firefighters get daily forecasts. However, there are tens of thousands of wildfires each year. AI programs help narrow down the list. The programs find out which fires could cause the most harm. That way, firefighters can respond to the most important fires first.

## WARNINGS

If fire risk is very high, forest workers may take action. They may not let people enter certain areas. They may warn people to be extra careful with campfires. They may even ban campfires. Also, stores may be banned from selling fireworks.

Signs let people know how high the fire risk is in certain areas.

## Chapter 5
# FIGHTING FIRES

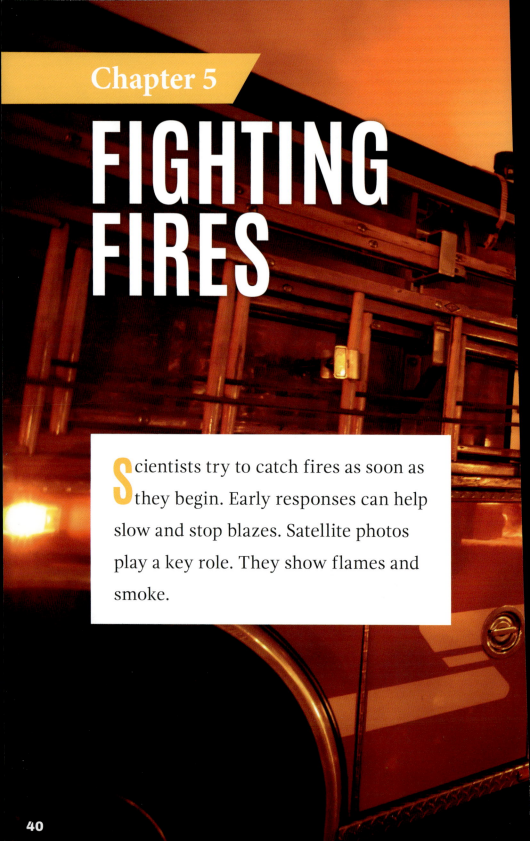

Scientists try to catch fires as soon as they begin. Early responses can help slow and stop blazes. Satellite photos play a key role. They show flames and smoke.

Firefighters try to reach wildfires quickly. Satellites can tell them where the fires are and how they're spreading.

Scientists also place sensors in forests. Some sensors measure chemicals. Some have heat-sensing cameras. Computer programs keep track of the measurements. The programs track when fires begin. Then, they tell firefighters. The programs may also send out warnings to the public.

## SMELLING WILDFIRES

Some sensors "smell" fires. The sensors take in air. They measure gases. They measure tiny particles. These sensors are 1,000 times more powerful than the smoke alarms in homes.

Scientists try to predict how wildfires will behave. Computer programs simulate wind and clouds. But fires can also change the weather. For instance, rising heat from a fire can make winds stronger. The programs try to predict all of these effects.

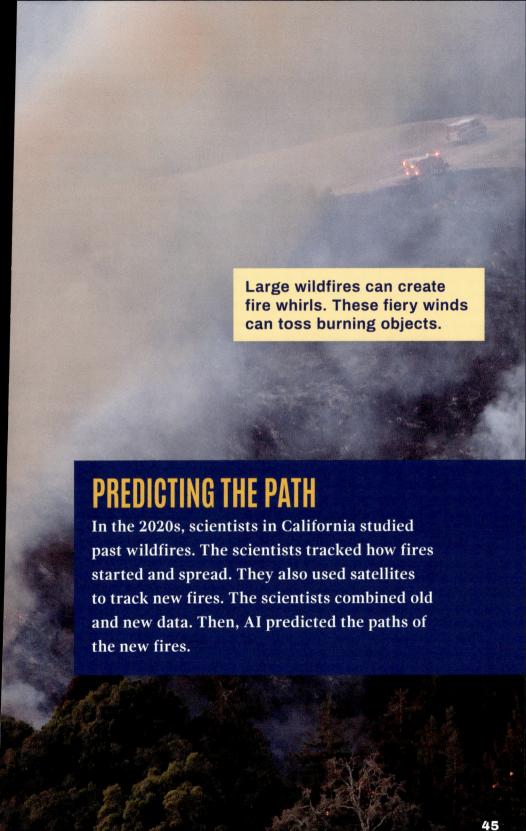

Large wildfires can create fire whirls. These fiery winds can toss burning objects.

## PREDICTING THE PATH

In the 2020s, scientists in California studied past wildfires. The scientists tracked how fires started and spread. They also used satellites to track new fires. The scientists combined old and new data. Then, AI predicted the paths of the new fires.

Scientists also track wildfires from airplanes. They fly directly over fires. They find the fires' edges. They also locate places with thick flames. The scientists use sensors that measure heat. They use this data to create maps. Then firefighters can view the maps from phones or tablets.

## THE BIG PICTURE

Wildfires can cover huge areas. Sometimes, several different wildfires happen at the same time. Data from airplanes and satellites gives scientists a big-picture view. That helps officials decide which places need help the most.

In 2018, a wildfire burned in northwestern Montana. Scientists used satellites to find the fire's edges.

# That's Wild!

# 2018 CAMP FIRE

In 2018, a power line snapped in Northern California. It started a huge wildfire. The blaze destroyed most of the town of Paradise. Thousands of people lost their homes. Harmful smoke spread throughout the state.

Scientists looked at data from satellites. They found out where the fire was strongest. And they studied smoke pollution. The scientists helped emergency response teams. They told the teams where to send help. They also warned people about bad air quality from the smoke.

**The Camp Fire burned 150,000 acres (60,700 ha) of forest.**

Chapter 6

# PREVENTING FUTURE FIRES

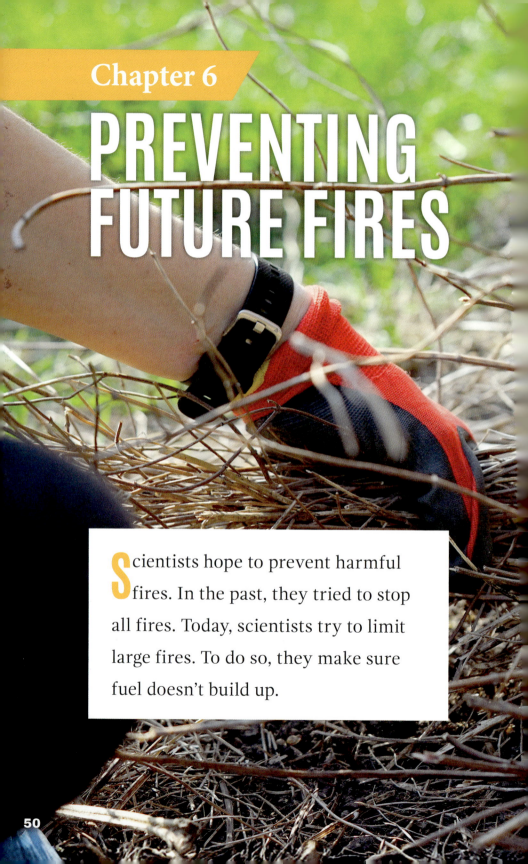

Scientists hope to prevent harmful fires. In the past, they tried to stop all fires. Today, scientists try to limit large fires. To do so, they make sure fuel doesn't build up.

People can protect their homes by removing nearby dead plants. That can slow the spread of wildfires.

Computer programs find areas where a fire could break out. Then, people can thin out forests. They can create firebreaks. People also carry out controlled burns. They work to keep forests safe and healthy.

**Roads can act as firebreaks.**

Early warnings can give people enough time to evacuate during wildfires.

Scientists hope to build more weather stations and better sensors. These will provide more data about forests and fires. Having more data is important. It helps scientists make better predictions.

## BETTER PREDICTIONS

European scientists are working on a big project. They want to predict wildfires anywhere on Earth. They use AI. The program uses maps and satellite data. It figures out how many dead plants are in an area. In 2024, the program predicted wildfires in Canada 10 days ahead of time.

Scientists also hope to learn more about long-term weather patterns. Climate change is affecting weather in several ways. So, wildfire experts work with climate scientists. They make long-term forecasts. They try to figure out which years may have more risk.

## LOS ANGELES FIRES

In January 2025, wildfires swept through Los Angeles, California. Scientists predicted the fires in advance. But it took weeks to contain the blazes. At least 29 people died. Thousands lost their homes.

Buildings go up in flames during the 2025 wildfires in Los Angeles, California.

# TIMELINE

**1850** — California bans controlled burns.

**1885** — The first official wildfire program in the United State is formed.

**1910** — Wildfires spread across huge parts of Montana, Idaho, and Washington.

**1944** — The United States Forest Service introduces Smokey Bear.

**1972** — Scientists develop a new system to map the risk of wildfires in an area.

**2005** — Members of the Southern Sierra Miwuk Nation and Tuolumne Band of Me-Wuk take part in a controlled burn in California.

**2018** — The Camp Fire spreads through large parts of Northern California. It destroys the town of Paradise.

**2024** — An AI program predicts wildfires in Canada 10 days ahead of time.

**2025** — Wildfires sweep through Los Angeles, California, leaving thousands of homes destroyed.

# COMPREHENSION QUESTIONS

*Write your answers on a separate piece of paper.*

1. Write a few sentences describing the main ideas of Chapter 3.

2. What do you think is the most important part of forecasting wildfires? Why?

3. What is the rarest type of wildfire?
    - A. crown fire
    - B. surface fire
    - C. ground fire

4. Why did people stop trying to put out all fires in the 1970s?
    - A. Too much oxygen was blowing through the forest.
    - B. Too much heat was causing forests to grow faster.
    - C. Too much fuel was building up on the ground.

**5.** What does **alert** mean in this book?

*The scientists act quickly. They **alert** a team of firefighters. Many homes are in the area. So, the firefighters must get there fast.*

    A. to tell someone about a problem
    B. to hide a problem from someone
    C. to make people disagree with each other

**6.** What does **contain** mean in this book?

*Firefighters use bulldozers to clear land. They also use hoses to shoot water at the flames. Within a few days, they **contain** the fire. The area's people and homes are safe.*

    A. avoid and ignore
    B. stop the spread of
    C. get closer to

*Answer key on page 64.*

# GLOSSARY

**colonists**
People who move to another area and take control.

**droughts**
Times of little or no rain.

**firebreaks**
Strips of land cleared of bushes and trees.

**humidity**
The amount of moisture in the air.

**ignite**
To catch fire.

**Indigenous**
Related to the original people who lived in an area.

**invasive**
Spreading quickly in a new area and causing many problems there.

**lasers**
Devices that shine strong beams of light.

**particles**
Tiny pieces of matter.

**predict**
To say what will happen in the future.

**satellite**
A device that orbits Earth, often to send or collect information.

**simulate**
To recreate certain conditions, often using a computer.

# TO LEARN MORE
## BOOKS

Jaycox, Jaclyn. *Wildfire: Inside the Inferno.* Capstone, 2023.

Murray, Julie. *Wildfires.* Abdo Publishing, 2025.

Ransom, Candice F. *Wildfires.* Apex Editions, 2023.

## ONLINE RESOURCES

Visit **www.apexeditions.com** to find links and resources related to this title.

## ABOUT THE AUTHOR

Dalton Rains is an author and editor from Saint Paul, Minnesota.

# INDEX

airplanes, 8, 46
artificial intelligence (AI), 35, 38, 45, 55

campfires, 13, 38
climate change, 56
controlled burns, 21, 23, 25, 27, 28, 53
crown fires, 19

data, 30, 32, 35, 38, 45–46, 48, 55
droughts, 17

firefighters, 6, 8, 15, 28, 38, 43, 46
forests, 4, 16–17, 21, 23, 38, 43, 48, 53, 55
fuel, 15, 19, 25, 27, 28, 32, 35–36, 50

ground fires, 19

Indigenous Americans, 21, 23, 28

lidar, 36
Los Angeles, California, 56

measurements, 35–36, 43

National Oceanic and Atmospheric Administration (NOAA), 7

oxygen, 15, 32

predicting, 30, 35, 44–45, 55–56

risk maps, 27, 38

satellites, 4, 6–7, 40, 45–46, 48, 55
sensors, 36, 43, 46, 55
Smokey Bear, 25
surface fires, 19

temperature, 7, 32, 35

United States Forest Service (USFS), 4, 25

weather stations, 32, 55

Yosemite National Park, 28

## ANSWER KEY:

1. Answers will vary; 2. Answers will vary; 3. C; 4. C; 5. A; 6. B